MAY   2017

SandCastle

Compound Words

tea + pot =
teapot

Amanda Rondeau

Consulting Editor Monica Marx, M.A./Reading Specialist

ABDO
Publishing Company

Published by SandCastle™, an imprint of ABDO Publishing Company, 4940 Viking Drive, Edina, Minnesota 55435.

Printed in the United States.

Credits
Edited by: Pam Price
Curriculum Coordinator: Nancy Tuminelly
Cover and Interior Design and Production: Mighty Media
Photo Credits: Comstock, Corbis Images, Eyewire Images, Hemera, ImageSource, PhotoDisc

Library of Congress Cataloging-in-Publication Data

Rondeau, Amanda, 1974-
    Tea + pot = teapot / Amanda Rondeau.
      p. cm. -- (Compound words)
    Includes index.
    Summary: Illustrations and easy-to-read text introduce compound words related to food and eating.
    ISBN 1-59197-441-0
    1. English language--Compound words--Juvenile literature. [1. English language--Compound words.] I. Title: Tea plus pot equals teapot. II. Title.

PE1175.R6694 2003
428.1--dc21

2003048109

SandCastle™ books are created by a professional team of educators, reading specialists, and content developers around five essential components that include phonemic awareness, phonics, vocabulary, text comprehension, and fluency. All books are written, reviewed, and leveled for guided reading, early intervention reading, and Accelerated Reader® programs and designed for use in shared, guided, and independent reading and writing activities to support a balanced approach to literacy instruction.

Let Us Know

After reading the book, SandCastle would like you to tell us your stories about reading. What is your favorite page? Was there something hard that you needed help with? Share the ups and downs of learning to read. We want to hear from you! To get posted on the ABDO Publishing Company Web site, send us e-mail at:

sandcastle@abdopub.com

SandCastle Level: Transitional

A compound word is two words joined together to make a new word.

tea + pot =

teapot

Elise has a tea party with her dad. She has a teapot and teacups.

stove + top =

stovetop

Danny's mom and aunt cook on the stovetop.

pea + nut =

peanut

Ellen's mom is making a peanut butter sandwich for her lunch.

table + cloth =

tablecloth

The Allens use a tablecloth for their family picnic.

dish + washer =

dishwasher

Gina helps her mom load the dishwasher.

tea + spoon =

teaspoon

Andi uses a
teaspoon when
she bakes.

No More Tea
for Wally

Bob and Bill sat down
for afternoon tea.

The tabletop looked just
as nice as could be.

Then Wally the cat upset
the teapot.

He slid on the tabletop
and took off like a shot.

Bob and Bill picked the
silverware up from the floor.

They said Wally can't come
to afternoon tea anymore.

More Compound Words

candlestick

coffeepot

cupboard

dinnertime

drugstore

icebox

nutcracker

placemat

potholder

saltshaker

saucepan

shopkeeper

supermarket

tablespoon

Thanksgiving

Glossary

afternoon   the part of the day from noon until sunset

dishwasher   a machine used to wash dishes

stovetop   the top of a stove that is used for cooking

tablecloth   a piece of fabric that is spread over a table to protect and decorate it

teapot   a covered pot with a spout and handle that is used for making and pouring tea

About SandCastle™

A professional team of educators, reading specialists, and content developers created the SandCastle™ series to support young readers as they develop reading skills and strategies and increase their general knowledge. The SandCastle™ series has four levels that correspond to early literacy development in young children. The levels are provided to help teachers and parents select the appropriate books for young readers.

Emerging Readers
(no flags)

Beginning Readers
(1 flag)

Transitional Readers
(2 flags)

Fluent Readers
(3 flags)

These levels are meant only as a guide. All levels are subject to change.

ABDO
Publishing Company

To see a complete list of SandCastle™ books and other nonfiction titles from ABDO Publishing Company, visit www.abdopub.com or contact us at:

4940 Viking Drive, Edina, Minnesota 55435 • 1-800-800-1312 • fax: 1-952-831-1632